T0004399

365 THINGS

EVERY HUNTER

SHOULD KNOW

STEVE CHAPMAN

TEN PEAKS PRESS™
EUGENE, OR

Portions of chapter 10 were adapted from *Character Sketches*, vols. I, II, III (Institute in Basic Life Principles). Used by permission.

Portions of chapter 14 were adapted from Steve Chapman, *The Good Husband's Guide to Balancing Hobbies and Marriage* (Eugene, OR: Harvest House Publishers, 2005). Used by permission.

Every effort has been made to give proper credit for all stories, poems, and quotations. If for any reason proper credit has not been given, please notify the author or publisher and proper notation will be given on future printing.

Cover design by Bryce Williamson

Cover image © PirahaPhotos, ednal, PREDRAGILIEVSKI, lushik, Tairy, aleksandarvelasevic / Getty Images

For bulk or special sales, please call 1 (800) 547-8979.
Email: Customerservice@hhpbooks.com

TEN PEAKS PRESS is a trademark of The Hawkins Children's LLC. Harvest House Publishers, Inc., is the exclusive licensee of the trademark TEN PEAKS PRESS.

365 THINGS EVERY HUNTER SHOULD KNOW

Copyright © 2008 by Steve Chapman
Published by Ten Peaks Press, an imprint of Harvest House Publishers
Eugene, Oregon 97408

ISBN-13 978-0-7369-8358-7 (Hardcover)
ISBN-10 0-7369-8359-4 (eBook)

Printed in China

22 23 24 25 26 27 28 / RDS-CD / 10 9 8 7 6 5 4 3 2 1

CONTENTS

INTRODUCTION

There are as many things hunters should know as there are hunters who should know them, and there's no way one person can cover them all. The booklet you hold in your hand contains short, pithy insights on hunting, biblical wisdom for life, and hunting lore for successful forays into the woods.

I've thoroughly enjoyed perusing my mind and heart as I reflected on hunts, stories, knowledge gleaned from others, and even a tall tale or two in my search for what to include. Whether you're a seasoned hunter or someone taking your first steps on this wonderful adventure, I hope you'll find some thoughts and suggestions that are meaningful, helpful, inspiring, encouraging, and that will even cause you to smile.

God bless all your seasons,
Steve Chapman

P.S. Many hunters are women…and that's great. For ease in writing I've used feminine pronouns when referring to spouses. Don't let that throw you if you're a woman! This book is written for you too.

QUOTES & QUIPS FOR HUNTERS

Insights to brighten your day and
bring to mind hunting seasons.

"To everything there is a season, *a time for every purpose under heaven"*
(Ecclesiastes 3:1).
The word "season" caught this hunter's eye!

"Throughout the city, the talk now is of the kill or the near kill. Some of it may even be true."
Jim Robbins, Helena, MT,
during hunting season

"For me, hunting is more than big antlers or shallow words. It's amber sunrises and the smell of leaves in an October forest. It's fluffy snowflakes landing on a cold gun barrel, and the smell of wet wool at the end of the day's hunt…In short, hunting is being there. It's experiencing all that nature has to offer."
Charles Alsheimer,
Whitetail Behavior Through the Seasons

"If a wife doesn't like what her husband likes to do as a hobby, then he's not doing it right."
ANNIE CHAPMAN

"To be successful at hunting, stay put just a little bit longer."
JAY HOUSTON

"The ending of deer season is a good thing. It reminds many of us that we have jobs— and we should return to them."
STEVE CHAPMAN

"Any relation to land—the habit of tilling it, or mining, or even hunting on it— generates the feeling of patriotism."
RALPH WALDO EMERSON

*"When you go to church and a trio sings, its nice.
But when the choir strikes up, ain't it grand!"*

BILLY, A RABBIT HUNTING GUIDE,
ON BRINGING 15 BEAGLES TO A HUNT

*"I saw the deer and took its life
then gave it to my skillful wife.
She added leeks and tall morels,
a secret spice I dare not tell
and deep red fruit of tomato vines,
legumes, and fire and evening time
bread of wheat and coffee hot...
She made me glad I took the shot!"*

STEVE CHAPMAN

*"When the sun is setting on a hunt and the
primer on my rifle cartridge is yet to be dented
by the firing pin, it's still been a good day."*

A WISE HUNTER

"Dogs have given us their absolute all. We are the center of their universe; we are the focus of their love and faith and trust. They serve us in return for scraps. It is without a doubt the best deal man has ever made."

ROGER CARAS

"You don't have to hunt to be a man, and you don't have to be a man to hunt."

STEVE CHAPMAN

"Some folks have said that my brother had very little patience. Well…I beg to differ. My brother had a ton of patience…if you were a deer or a fish!"

MARK KERSTETTER, IN A EULOGY FOR HIS BROTHER, ALAN

"Action without thought is like shooting without aim."

AMERICAN PROVERB

"The dog of ambition hunts best unleashed."
STEVE CHAPMAN

"Until the lions have historians, tales of the hunt will always glorify the hunter."
AFRICAN PROVERB

"A duck blind is a bedroom where its temporary dwellers rest their souls and dream of future hunts. It's home…and I like going there."
STEVE CHAPMAN

"Rule one at elk camp: If the huntin' is good, supper will probably come out of a can. The steaks only come out when the huntin' is in the tank."
JAY HOUSTON

"It takes one to hunt one."
ANNIE CHAPMAN, ON TURKEY HUNTING

"Bass Pro and Cabelas are not churches."
DON HICKS

"There is a poignancy, a tinge of sadness intermingled with the exhilaration of a successful hunt, that has the aura of sacredness. Confronting these feelings, the paradoxical counterpoise of life and death, loss in the midst of capture, is funda-mental to how and why I am a hunter."*
MARY ZEISS STANGE

* I'm not sure I fully understand this quote, but it sounds good.

"No, I'm not a good shot, but I shoot often."
THEODORE ROOSEVELT

"Are you going to get Nathan one of those 21s?"*
ANNIE CHAPMAN

* She meant .22s, of course.

"As I reflect back to my youth, I feel blessed to have grown up in the country. Farm life could be hard, but being surrounded by nature had a way of easing the strain. Roaming the wild haunts of my parents' farm was always special. In many ways, it gave me a foundation for the values that guide me today."

CHARLES ALSHEIMER, *WHITETAIL: RIGHTS OF AUTUMN*

"Hunting is one of those pleasures that you won't understand if you have to have it explained, which is good because folks who enjoy it can't fully explain why."

RON SPOMER, "WHY HUNT," *WILDLIFE ART NEWS*

"Physical bravery is an animal instinct; moral bravery is much higher and truer courage."

WENDELL PHILLIPS

"The deer you're hunting are smart critters. If you want to get an arrow into one of the mature whitetails, you'll have to take your climber further back into the woods."

MARK SMITH, ON WHY I COULDN'T
GET A DEER AT MY FIELD-EDGE STAND

"Never go cheap on boots. There's far too much stacked on top of them."

JAY HOUSTON

"To be sure of hitting the target, shoot first, and call whatever you hit the target."

ASHLEIGH BRILLIANT

"Permission to hunt someone's property is not an invitation to hunt their neighbor's."

JASON CRUISE, *THE HEART OF THE SPORTSMAN*

"Just because we hunters might go home with an unpunched tag doesn't mean we're leaving the woods skunked. There have been times when I've left the stand with the memory of a sunrise so lovely that I was reminded to say a quiet 'thank You' to the Creator. Is that a trophy? You bet!"

STEVE CHAPMAN

"And early morn I slowly rise to go and face the beast,
I race against the new sun rising in the east,
I'll one last time look slowly back
to view my earthly home
and to the darkened room on the second
floor where my lover sleeps alone,
and slowly take that final turn
that leads to my best place,
where many times I through the years
have made my hunting chase,
my bow or gun I slowly place upon
earth's dew-drenched clover,
and listen close till evening says,
'For now the hunt is over.'"

DON HICKS

"It's amazing how much effort I can put into making
myself feel totally disappointed and depressed."

STEVE CHAPMAN,
AFTER SEARCHING FOR A WOUNDED DEER

"My childhood fire was lit by the graceful figure
of a mature buck running across a plowed field
on our farm. That fire has kept me heading
back to the woods for more than 45 years."

CHARLES ALSHEIMER,
HUNTING WHITETAILS BY THE MOON

"Hunt with a son when he is young and you
won't have to hunt for him when he is older."

AUTHOR UNKNOWN

"Those who spend the most time looking for game
seem to be the ones doing most of the finding!"

JAY HOUSTON

"If we banned hunting as we know it today,
there would be no crops in a short five years."

CONSERVATION OFFICER

"When I see the sunrise I think of you,
how you're faithful and true to me
And when I hear the bluebird's morning refrain,
I hear your name so lovely."

STEVE CHAPMAN, WRITTEN TO ANNIE
(FEEL FREE TO PRESENT THIS TO YOUR SPOUSE.
THIS MAY HELP EASE YOUR MATE'S FRUSTRATION
ABOUT YOUR MANY TRIPS TO THE WOODS. FOR THE
REST OF THE LYRIC SEE "SONG OF THE HUNTER" IN MY BOOK
A HUNTER SETS HIS SIGHTS.)

"If you have no sense of remorse after taking the life
of an animal, you're not a hunter, you're a killer."

STEVE CHAPMAN, ADVICE TO MY SON

"The only reason I played golf was so that I
could afford to go hunting and fishing."

SAM SNEAD

*"The bird hunting a locust is unaware
of the hawk hunting him."*
ANCIENT PROVERB

*"Show me a kid who can sit still for three or
four hours and wait patiently for a deer to
appear, and I'll show you a youngster who
has the seed of greatness growing inside."*
STEVE CHAPMAN

*"Hunting is not a sport. In a sport, both sides
should know they are in the game."*
PAUL RODRIQUEZ

*"After eating an entire bull, a mountain lion felt
so good he started roaring. He kept it up until
a hunter came along and shot him. The moral:
When you're full of bull, keep your mouth shut."*
WILL ROGERS

"The easiest I've ever fallen asleep the night before going hunting was just before my first hunt. I simply didn't know any better."
STEVE CHAPMAN

"The first one was really exciting indeed…but it's not anything like getting your last one."
A DAD, ON HIS LAST HUNT WITH HIS SON

"The most vulnerable animals that can be hunted are the ones that allow themselves to be patterned. In the same way, if we keep entering the woods of our spiritual lives every day in the same exact place because we believe ritual equals righteousness, sooner or later our feathers are gonna fly."
STEVE CHAPMAN,
ANOTHER LOOK AT LIFE FROM A DEER STAND

"If someone is mistaken for a moose and is shot, he or she is probably better off anyway!"
ANONYMOUS (AND RIGHTLY SO)

"A drawn bow is a stick nine-tenths broken."
JIM HAMM

"Skilled bowyers will agree that a perfect bow never begins with a perfect stave. Instead, the key to a great shooting bow is in the amount of understanding the bowyer has of the wood and the level of his or her ability to work with it. Human lives are similar. They have their 'knots and twists,' imperfections that God, the 'Heavenly Bowyer,' has to know how to work around."
STEVE CHAPMAN,
ANOTHER LOOK AT LIFE FROM A DEER STAND

"Be still, and know that I am God."
PSALM 46:10, MY FAVORITE VERSE
WHEN ON A DEER STAND

2

SECRETS FROM A SEASONED HUNTER

Observations to improve
your hunting skills.

A barbed wire fence can offer the best evidence of the presence of critters in the area. Elk, deer, bear, and old hippies leave behind remnants of their tresses as they crawl under or between the wires.

T hunder is a turkey hunter's friend. A "hot" male during springtime mating season often gobbles when the thunder rolls, giving away his location. But be careful if lightning comes. Your gun can act as a lightning rod, bringing a massive electrical charge directly to where you're standing.

S quirrels are curious creatures. If you're hunting bushytails and one escapes into a hole in a tree, sit down on the ground on the opposite side of the hole and quietly wait for 20 minutes or so. You'll probably see the squirrel again!

Deer take the line of least resistance when traveling. Before hunting season, cut a trail across a field of heavy grass or brush, wait a week, and then check the trail for tracks. Hopefully you'll be surprised by how much your "trail trap" is used. Put a stand nearby and enjoy the traffic.

If you're walking through the woods on the way to your deer stand and your presence causes a squirrel or chipmunk to squawk and nervously run for cover, don't be overly concerned that the resident deer are spooked. Small critters like squirrels and chipmunks act the same way when hawks and owls fly over their territory. Deer may hear the squawking and be curious about the cause, but if you stop walking for a few minutes and let the little creatures settle down, more than likely the deer in the area will relax too.

If you jump a deer or even a few deer on the way to your stand, don't fret. Remember they're the only deer you disturbed. Mount your stand and quietly wait for the other deer in the area to come by. The spooked ones may return too.

When building a ground blind, make the cover in front of you multidimensional. Start about 12 to 15 feet out and place limbs and brush every 3 feet until you come to your seat. Avoid building a solid wall of cover. It won't look natural to an animal's eyes.

When hunting on the ground, make sure there is plenty of structure behind you so your silhouette won't alert game to your presence. Also make sure the wind is in your face.

As bothersome as they can be, noisy planes over-head can be useful. When the leaves are extra dry and crunchy under your feet as you're slipping into position for a shot, a plane can provide sound cover.

When deer hunting, don't despair when dogs are barking in the distance. Instead, get ready with your gun or bow. Game may be running toward you.

If time allows, never exit a deer stand when deer are nearby. Doing so might give them something you'd rather they didn't have—an education.

Don't walk directly on an active deer trail. When you can, walk at least five feet away. Also, if at all possible, avoid having your skin or clothing touch branches that hang at a deer's nose level. A deer's sensitive nose will pick up the scents and put it on guard.

When retrieving a deer or any other four-footed animal you've connected with using gun or bow, remember the basics. If the critter falls in your field of vision, wait in your stand and watch the body for 10 minutes. Have your weapon ready in case it stands up. If you hear the animal crash to the ground but it's out of sight, wait 30 minutes before going for retrieval. If the animal runs out of sight and you don't hear a crash, force yourself to wait at least an hour or, better yet, two, before tracking. This way the animal won't run far. You also don't want to get too close to a wounded animal. Give your shot time to do its work.

Always reload immediately after a muzzle loader shot. You'll be glad you took this precaution if the animal you thought was mortally wounded suddenly stands up and runs.

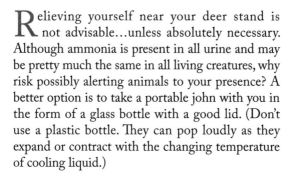

During a full moon, try hunting deer from 10 AM to 2 PM. Deer often bed at daylight and stir with hunger midmorning.

Relieving yourself near your deer stand is not advisable...unless absolutely necessary. Although ammonia is present in all urine and may be pretty much the same in all living creatures, why risk possibly alerting animals to your presence? A better option is to take a portable john with you in the form of a glass bottle with a good lid. (Don't use a plastic bottle. They can pop loudly as they expand or contract with the changing temperature of cooling liquid.)

A predawn arrival into turkey area often yields the pleasurable sound of gobbling birds. But if the hen population is significant in the area, very likely all you'll enjoy is the music of gobbling. Once the toms find the hens, getting them to come to you is very difficult. Their motto is "Love the one you're with." So enjoy your sleep and hunt the gobblers from 9 AM to 2 PM. During these hours the hens are likely nesting, leaving the gobblers lonely and love-sick. Unrequited love may compel them to respond to your turkey call.

The excitement of seeing your quarry approach may knock the rudiments of shooting out of your brain. As soon as you feel your heart rate rise, rehearse the steps to a well-placed shot. In fact, why not rehearse the scenario at the shooting range. Pretend a trophy animal is coming in. When the situation happens in real life and adrenalin begins to flow, you'll be ready.

When a deer in a herd is arrowed, sometimes the other deer linger with the wounded one. If this happens, stand still until the unharmed deer move on. While you wait, make good use of their presence. Study their behavior and mentally log the info for later use. If you're in a treestand and out of sight of the deer, practice your draw (without an arrow, of course). Make sure you don't release the string—a dry fire—so you don't permanently damage the bow.

Using a treestand with protective rails while archery hunting requires care so you don't slap the rail with the bow limb. Leaning slightly over the rail is usually the solution…as long as you're tethered to the tree with a full-body safety harness.

If there are cedar or pine trees in the area you're hunting, snap off a small branch and rub it vigorously between your gloves. The scent provides a natural and effective cover.

Vanilla extract and acorns have similar smells.

When the sun is shining in the eyes of a game animal, you have a distinct advantage. This is a good time to stalk or move if necessary to take your shot.

When the sky is clear, be sure to set up in the morning and evening so the big yellow ball on the horizon doesn't blind you.

Don't buy new boots a day or two before going on a hunt that requires a good deal of walking. Buy the boots at least 30 days before departure and break them in. Why? Because "barking dogs" bite!

Deer often follow the same trail in and out of a bedding area. If you're morning hunting and see a buck in the distance slipping through the woods on the way to a thicket, mentally mark the spot where the trail might be. Wait a little while and quietly move your stand to that area. Return early enough that evening to rendezvous with the deer as it retraces its steps to a feeding area. Make sure you're downwind of the bedding area.

Hang a deer vertically as quickly as possible after a kill and let it stay there for a while. This allows a maximum amount of blood to drain. This important step in preparing for butchering helps keep the meat at its highest quality.

When shooting an arrow, the sound of the "collapsing" limbs as the arrow is released may cause an alert deer to "jump the string." It drops several inches as it prepares to spring away. If your shot is aimed high, the arrow will fly over the deer's back. To avoid this problem aim at the lower portion of the deer's chest cavity or get a quieter bow.

When shooting an arrow at a target below your stand, remember the "10:30 rule." Keep your back straight and bend at the waist, making your body look like the hands of a clock position at 10:30. This puts your release stance in the same position you normally use when target practicing.

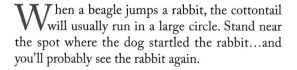

When a beagle jumps a rabbit, the cottontail will usually run in a large circle. Stand near the spot where the dog startled the rabbit...and you'll probably see the rabbit again.

When a weather front is moving in, deer usually feed, even in the middle of the day. Think of humans running to the grocery store to stock up when a snowstorm is approaching. If conditions allow (no lightning, for example) and you're prepared for foul weather, stay in your stand and look for emerging deer.

When you make a "contact call"—attempting to entice an unseen animal to you—using a rattling rack or grunt call for deer, a bugle call for elk, or a turkey call, even if you don't see an animal respond right away, be patient. Keeping the calling instrument in your hand while waiting for animals to appear will help you stay alert.

When a heavy cloud cover is forecast for your morning hunt, you potentially have an extra 20 minutes or so of darkness to use as concealment when slipping into a stand. That translates into a little bit of extra sleep if needed.

I've seen deer stay just on the dark side of the shadow cast by a tree line or mountain ridge as it progresses down a field during sunset. Setting a stand further up the field made the difference between having plenty of shooting light and running out of legal light when they showed up.

Turkeys love to "dust" themselves to lessen the number of bugs they deal with. A dusting area isn't hard to spot. It's usually a three- to five-foot circle of bare earth, slightly indented and powdery in appearance. There should be plenty of turkey tracks around it. If you want to enjoy a long sit outdoors and ambush some birds, set up at a dusting area at daylight and wait until noon or one o'clock.

Camouflage clothes are popular today and many kinds are available. Choosing the most suitable outfit for your hunt isn't hard. The key is the shades, not the patterns. If the leaves are on the trees and the woods are dark because sunlight is almost completely blocked, wear a dark shade of camo. If the leaves are off the trees and the woods are light, use lighter camo. If there's snow on the ground, camo with some white in it is perfect. While camouflage clothing is great to have, remember that in bygone years many deer were taken by hunters wearing blue jeans and red plaid wool shirts.

You've been invited to a hunting camp. On the first day out you walk to a remote area and spot a sizable deer, but it's out of range. That night do you bring up the sighting? If you mention it, chances are very good that the next day someone else in the group will head to "your" spot. I'm speaking from experience. You can read about this and many more hunts in my book *A Look at Life from a Deer Stand*.

One of the hazards of modern, high-tech compound bows is that very little tuning is needed to keep them shooting accurately. This manufacturing accomplishment may lull you into believing you don't need to practice as much. Not true. The bow needs to be used to stay in good condition, and your muscles need to be strengthened and toned. Although it's sometimes tempting to start shooting a week or two before hunting season, it's best to shoot year round. Keeping your equipment—including your body—in great shape helps make hunts productive and fun. And when you can place a shot accurately, you lessen the suffering of the animals you're hunting.

"Still hunting" is slipping very quietly and slowly through the woods, stopping often to look and listen for your game animal. Stalking is very similar except you know there is an animal nearby. Still hunting can give birth to a stalk. Because I keep all my senses tuned to their highest level while moving through the woods, its amazing how exhausting an hour or two of hunting is. But it's a very satisfying tired! If I'm not worn out at the end of the day I know I haven't given it my all.

A great way to hone your skill of estimating distances is to use tennis balls as archery targets. I put claw-type tips on my arrows—the kind that will grab dirt and keep an arrow from driving underground—and start throwing tennis balls into the yard. Because they stop at random distances I calculate the range and then check my accuracy by taking the shots. Try it. It's a lot of fun and very productive.

When a critter is close and you need to alter your bow or gun position to get a shot, timing is everything. Be patient. Wait until the animal can't see you before you move. Perhaps it will move behind a tree, another animal will block the line of sight momentarily, the turkey turns so tail feathers block the view, or a deer lowers its head to feed. If there are several animals, learn to watch them all at the same time. This skill takes practice, so keep trying. You can do it!

There's usually a feeling of regret when a "button buck," or yearling, is killed because the hunter thought it was a doe. The deer doesn't get to grow to trophy size or become mature enough to sire many offspring. I've done this in the past. Now I know that older deer have longer faces and noses. By watching many deer and studying photos, I can now usually tell when a nose or face seems short. I encourage you to develop this skill. Then, when you see a deer with a short nose or face, you'll know it's still young and let it walk.

My choice of boot when bow hunting is rubber high-top. When I need to replace a pair of rubber boots, I don't buy new just before the season begins. Rubber can have a residual odor that may alert deer. So I buy boots at least a month ahead and wear them often to the woods to "season" the exterior.

***

Get over bad shots. Errant shots and silly mistakes made during hunting season sometimes result in not bagging the trophy of a lifetime or, worse, a wounded animal that couldn't be found. If you have a tendency, like I do, to mentally replay these unfortunate moments, turn your regret into something constructive. Examine what was done wrong and figure out what you'll do differently next time. Hindsight is 20/20 only if it makes the road ahead clearer.

3

INESCAPABLE
HUNTING TRUTHS

Pithy insights for every hunter.

Aching in the derriere is at its most uncomfortable level seconds before a huge gobbler appears.

Game wardens only ask to see your license when you've left it at home.

Even when no wind in the morning woods is apparent, one lone leaf will find that unde-tectable rising thermal. Its dancing motion in your peripheral vision will make you tense up and look in its direction over and over again. The temptation to shoot the leaf will be strong…but fight it! Save your ammo.

Game usually appears after you've poured a cup of hot coffee, bit into an apple, opened a candy bar, or prepared for bladder relief. Unfortunately, deliberately doing any of these activities doesn't attract them.

When deer hunting, a lot of turkeys are usually sighted. When turkey hunting, plenty of deer are seen. When the seasons overlap and you have a tag for either critter, you usually don't see anything.

Mosquitoes seem to sense the elevated heart rate of a hunter watching an approaching animal. The thudding drumbeat is their cue to swarm in...and invite their friends to the blood buffet.

Hunting and golf are a lot alike. In both cases, you go to the woods to look for something.

Uncontrollable shivers caused by extremely low temperatures usually start just before the biggest buck you've ever seen steps into your field of view.

Because you forgot to change it to silent mode, your cell phone will ring at the first sign of deer movement.

The obnoxious, excited cawing of crows often tells you turkeys are nearby. Be ready!

No matter how long you boil antlers, they're still crunchy when you bite into them.

Deer, elk, bear, and other animals hanging in your trophy room don't talk, support you, or love you—no matter how much you talk about or to them. Every married person or family member obsessed with hunting should keep this in mind.

There is no softer pillow than a clear conscience. Remember this when the temptation to hunt out of season has you in its sights.

A candy bar has no calories or fat grams when consumed in a treestand. Unfortunately they mysteriously appear the minute your feet are back on the ground.

Someone else always gets the biggest deer in your county, and it never helps to pack up and move.

The first deer taken is always the biggest.

When on a group hunt, someone is usually dangerously allergic to dander in deer fur. Inevitably your name will be drawn to hunt with that person.

Words, bullets, and arrows have something in common. Once they're sent, you can't get them back.

I can't remember one moment of boredom while on a deer stand, sitting against a tree during gobbler season, walking the mountains in search of elk, or sitting in a duck blind. Hunting is exciting anticipation followed by thorough satisfaction (whether game is bagged or not).

All deer look bigger through a peep sight.

Rain storms and blood trails often show up at the same time.

Every hunter, at some point, leaves something in the woods he desperately needs and cherishes. Items range from a great sounding, well-seasoned box call left next to a bush during turkey season to a foursome of perfectly tuned arrows in a detachable quiver left hanging on a tree limb. Your heart won't rest until you return for your treasure. This might be as close as some hunters can come to understanding how God views and values the souls among us who are lost in the woods of this life.

DON HICKS, PARAPHRASED

4

SURVIVING THE HUNT

Good reminders about keeping safe.

If you go hunting alone, always let someone know where you're going or write the information down and leave it in a conspicuous place. If you decide to change your plans in the field, call someone and let them know where you're going. If no phone is available, leave a note on your vehicle's dash—in plain sight—regarding your altered plans.

If you're hunting with a friend or in a group for rabbit, grouse, duck, or quail, be proactive about gun safety. If no one steps forward to audibly remind everyone to check the safeties on their guns after a flurry of shots, don't hesitate to speak up. A willingness to make safety a priority saves lives.

Don't be shy about confronting irresponsible behaviors or attitudes in fellow hunters the first time you notice them. Waiting could be deadly.

Before field dressing an arrowed deer, make sure you know where the broadhead is. If the shot was a pass through, the arrow should be easily found. If the broadhead has replaceable blades, make sure all the blades are still connected. If the arrow didn't pass through, assume it's still in the animal. If you don't see the arrow after you recover the carcass, the shaft may have broken off, leaving the broadhead inside the deer. You don't want to unexpectedly encounter the razor sharp blades when you dress the deer. Severing your tendons, muscles, or blood vessels will ruin your good hunt.

Whether hunting alone or with another person, never cross a fence holding your weapon. Lay your gun on the ground a few feet up or down the fence row with the muzzle facing away from you and the butt of the gun slightly protruding on the other side. This allows you to pull the gun under the fence with the business end pointed away. If your weapon is a bow, don't cross with a knocked arrow. If your quiver is shoulder or waist mounted, remove it and set it on the ground.

If you use a gun with a mounted scope, make sure there is sufficient distance between your eye and the rear rim of the scope's eyepiece. Otherwise the recoil could result in bloody wounds on both ends of the gun.

While it's acceptable to scope an animal you're hunting, using the scope to view houses, cars, or humans is never wise. Pack binoculars for spotting people, locations, and objects.

Using a full-body tethering harness while in a treestand minimizes injuries, saves lives, and reassures loved ones you hunt safely.

Blaze orange is a hunter's best friend. Never leave home without it. Even during archery deer season or turkey season, when it's not required by law, placing a square of blaze orange on an animal being removed from the woods is a smart thing to do.

Avoid putting a loaded rifle in a scabbard, especially when it's mounted on a saddle or ATV.

Having a loaded gun inside a vehicle is dangerous. Feet, legs, toes, and eardrums are a few body parts that could suffer gravely from a weapon discharged in a truck cab. Add to that pricey transmissions, crankcases, and other expensive mechanical items that might get hit by an errant bullet, and you have great reasons to ask everyone to unload their weapons before entering your rig.

Attempting to remove a lodged bullet, shotgun shell, or muzzle loader charge from the forward end of a gun barrel is a wacky idea. The projectile is meant for animal flesh, not human. To avoid accidental discharge, take the gun to a gunsmith.

Always wear ear protection at a firing range when sighting in a gun or plinking around. "WHAT?" "I SAID, 'ALWAYS WEAR EAR PROTECTION AT A FIRING RANGE.'"

Invest in the type of climbing harnesses used by loggers and telephone pole workers. Using a high-quality harness when preparing trees for your climbing stands makes the job safer and easier due to the freedom to use both hands. The expenditure will be worth every dime you'll never see again.

Every hunter's day pack should contain these safety items:

- *Referee whistle:* For letting others know where you are or to call a time out if your buddies are fighting over the last sandwich.
- *Tourniquet:* If you get hurt you can stop the bleeding until you get medical help or finish hunting.
- *Cell phone:* For emergency calls, such as to a counselor who can talk you through the depression caused by a missed shot.
- *Bottle of water:* For rehydration and, after the bottle is empty, for "de-hydrating" while in a deer stand.
- *Matches:* In case you need to build a fire to get warm, use as protection, or to let folks in helicopters know your location 'cause you forgot your compass.
- *Utility knife:* One with a fold-out four-wheeler attachment would be really nice.
- *Hot pink ribbon:* For tracking a wounded animal, leaving trail markers if you get lost, and to prove you're secure in your manhood.
- *Space-age blanket:* The kind you've always wondered if it really keeps you warm, but it looks good in your pack and is light and compact. (Yes, they do work.)
- *Energy bar:* For emergency nourishment...or a snack on that two-hour hunt behind the house.

Make it a strict rule to leave a treestand at the first sign of falling ice or freezing rain, whether you're in a permanently mounted or a portable type.

Test your waders *before* duck or goose season. You don't want to get out there and experience a frigid, sickness-inducing, breath-taking, hunt-ending liquid surprise. If your waders are getting really worn, purchase new ones. Better new waders than prescription medicines.

At home always separate guns and ammo, and store both behind lock and key. This policy is essential when children are present or may be present.

If you're not sure the area beyond the animal you want to shoot is clear of humans, houses, vehicles, or unwanted targets, don't take the shot—no matter how difficult it is to let the opportunity pass. An ounce of doubt may spare you a ton of regret.

When pursuing wild turkey in the spring or deer in the early part of archery season, disease-carrying ticks can be a troublesome and dangerous nemesis in some areas. A good repellent is a valuable defense, but don't forgo a thorough self-examination after a hunt. For married hunters, asking a spouse to perform the "tick check" can be the very best result of a day in the woods. Know the dangers of tick bites and the telltale signs of them.

Tips for tick removal: Never squeeze the body of a tick. You don't want the disease-laden contents of the body pushed into your flesh. Once the tick is pinched properly, pull it out quickly. Taking too much time may cause the tick to become agitated and regurgitate it's stomach contents into you—a very gross proposition. Don't pull on the body; always make sure you grasp the head.

If you must wade across a stream that has a rocky bed, unload your weapon. Carefully test each stone for stability and slipperiness before putting your full weight on it.

There are far too many treestand accidents each year, and some are deadly. While ascending or descending a treestand, make each movement a deliberate action. Broken bones and loved one's broken hearts often begin with a hunter's broken concentration.

Never "dry fire" a compound bow. It could literally explode and do great physical harm to you and anyone nearby. Even when pulling a compound bow to full draw to test draw length or for any other purpose, mount an arrow on the string just in case the bow accidentally releases. The arrow will provide enough resistance to keep the limbs from responding too violently. The safest place to test a bow is outside facing a solid target. If done inside, use proper precautions or go to an archery range.

Never hoist a loaded gun or strung bow with a pull-string to an elevated stand. And don't use the trigger guard as the tie-on point for your hoisting rope.

If you're planning to return to elevated stands permanently mounted in a tree or on a tripod, remember the dangerous "R's": *rot* and *rust*. Home-made wooden stands, commercially manufactured stands, and kit-built stands are vulnerable to these two culprits. Closely inspect permanent perches *before* opening day to ensure a good, safe hunt.

When someone hands you a pistol, even if he tells you it's not loaded, consider it loaded until you personally check. This assumption saves lives.

Drugs of any kind (legal and illegal) and guns go together like gasoline and sparks.

If the condition of a harvested animal looks even slightly suspicious (signs of disease, infections, etc.) don't eat the meat. It's better to be safe than sick. Notify your local wildlife management office or agency of the problem, and if possible, take the questionable carcass to them for inspection.

Know what to do if you're bitten by a snake so if it happens you won't panic and make your heart race, which would pump the venom through your body faster. Poisonous snakes, if common to your area, are another good reason to carry a cell phone or hunt with a friend.

In case you disturb a nest of bees while setting up or moving a deer stand, carry an "insect bomb" or fogger. Make sure it's within easy reach. In fact, practice grabbing it before your journey into the summer or early fall woods. If you disturb a nest and the bees or hornets swarm, quickly detonate the bomb. Wave it in circles around you while being careful to hold your breath. I'm sure I don't have to tell you to quickly exit the area! (Remember not to litter. Take the bomb with you when you leave or return for it after dark.)

If you leave your treestand harness in a permanently mounted stand, inspect it before each season and often during the season. Belt seams, hard plastic buckles, and metal chains are good places to check for torn threads, dry rot, rust, and wear and tear. Some of nature's harshest enemies to a cloth harness are time, a damp environment, growth of the tree, and gnawing critters such as squirrels. In most cases replace the harness if wear is apparent. A new unit is much cheaper than a helicopter ride to an emergency room.

Wear heavy-duty, elbow-length rubber gloves when field dressing a deer. Some bacteria in the blood of animals are very unfriendly to the human system.

Learn what poison ivy, poison oak, and other common poisonous plants in your hunting area look like. If you come into contact with a poison leaf or vine, as soon as possible wash the skin thoroughly with cold water and soap. Keep a supply of a product called Tecnu on hand. It does the best job I've seen in neutralizing the poisonous oily substance.

Treestand tether devices that are secured only around the waist are dangerous. Studies show they can cause the wearer to flip upside down, risking suffocation. Even if you don't flip, a waist-only harness may slip up and compress the rib cage, seriously impairing breathing. A full body harness is the best investment.

A safety-conscious hunter recognizes the similarity between a razor-sharp knife and a policeman. Both are wonderful friends—as long as you respect them.

When turkey hunting in the spring season, never wear red, white, or pale blue. These three colors are commonly seen on the head of a gobbler during mating season due to the blood flow caused by his "mating urges." You don't want to be mistaken for a male turkey. (Or be chased by a female turkey!)

Also, when leaving the woods with a deceased turkey, wearing blaze orange may save your life.

If you've had a gun in storage since the previous season, clean the gun before firing. This will remove any rust that may have formed and any other debris or obstructions that may have gotten into the barrel.

Avoid using a climbing stand in a hard bark tree, even if that particular tree is in the very best location in the area you want to hunt. If the bark is too hard, the teeth that hold the stand securely to the tree may not sink in enough and suddenly…or gradually…lose their grip, causing you to plummet to the cold, hard ground.

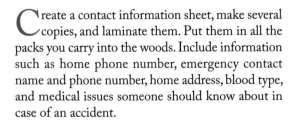

Create a contact information sheet, make several copies, and laminate them. Put them in all the packs you carry into the woods. Include information such as home phone number, emergency contact name and phone number, home address, blood type, and medical issues someone should know about in case of an accident.

If lightning occurs while you're hunting and you're carrying a gun, keep in mind that it's made of metal. You're basically carrying a lightning rod. Unload it and hurry out of the woods with the barrel pointed to the ground.

I just returned from a ride through the country on my motorcycle. I was reminded that whatever time of day it is, deer have a tendency to get up and feed just before a storm front moves through. If you mount your metal pony and head down roads in deer-populated areas when dark clouds are moving in, grip a little tighter, keep your eyes moving like radar, and slow down. This goes for driving in regular rigs too. "Grilled venison" is not the best way to fill your tag.

Avoid walking over rough terrain or unstable ground with an arrow on your bow string. If you fall you might skewer yourself. When stalking an animal or approaching an animal that has been wounded, take every step slowly and with alert deliberation, planting your feet firmly before shifting your weight.

If you wear white T-shirts as undergarments, don't forget to button your camo shirt all the way to the top. The brilliant white glow of exposed cotton can be seen far away, and an eager hunter may think he's seeing a whitetail deer or a hot gobbler's head. The best solution is to wear green, beige, or gray undergarments.

Make sure your quarry is dead before putting your hands on it. Poke it with a gun barrel, an arrow, or gently kick it. Be careful! After doing a poke test, a gentleman in Nebraska put his bow and quiver on the ground and gripped the antlers of a ten-point buck. He was quite surprised when the deer suddenly revived. Fearing the agitated animal would attack him, the hunter decided his safest choice was to hold on until the weakening creature died. After a minute or two of extreme "buck wrestling," the deer finally succumbed. The exhausted hunter vowed to be more careful in the future.

If you use archery equipment most of the time, when you do use a gun remember to check the safety. With most gun hunters, checking the safety is habitual, but avid archers may overlook that safety feature.

If you ascend a tree with a portable climbing stand but need to trim some branches to clear the area for making a shot, attach your safety harness to the tree first. I remember the day I used a small handsaw on a branch that obstructed my view. It was about 4 inches in diameter and 12 feet long. Because it was full of foliage, it was heavy. My plan was to cut it and let it fall to the ground. But when the cut was three quarters done, the weight of the branch caused it to partially snap. Because it was still attached to the tree it violently swung toward me and nearly knocked me off the stand. I won't make that mistake again!

When rabbit hunting with friends but without dogs, the typical method is to line up shoulder to shoulder several yards apart and press through the brush to kick up cottontails. Make sure you keep the hunters on either side of you in sight, especially when pushing through dense cover. Also make sure everyone is wearing blaze orange and talks or uses whistles. In the excitement of spying a rabbit, be careful not to track the rabbit with your gun by swinging it off to your side or behind you.

5

HUNTING LORE

Thoughts to encourage you
and keep you trouble-free.

Hunting is not like fishing in one particular and profound way. Fishing can be catch and release. Hunting is catch and consume only. Hunters go to the woods and fields with the intent to render permanent harm to their prey. You can't shoot an animal, hold it and admire it for a moment, and then let it go scampering back into the wild. Because the sole purpose of hunting is to kill to eat, serious consideration should be given when describing it...and what is fun (the time outdoors, the sighting of game, the stalk, the skill) and what is pure business (the kill).

If you're drawn to the intense challenge of finding and outwitting the wary creatures of the earth (such as deer, turkey, elk, and other edibles), you possess character traits that will serve you well in other areas of life: patience (long waits on a deer stand), determination (a sustained stalk), boldness (asking a land owner for permission to hunt), courage (ascending high into trees), endurance (sitting for hours in the cold), and a sense of rightness (hitting the target).

Put your family first…yes, even before hunting. What does it profit you if you have the biggest trophy rack on the planet but lose your family in the process of bagging it? Even if you get the number one trophy in the world, in your state, in your town, at your deer camp, it's just one pull of the trigger from being replaced. Families are irreplaceable.

As a hunter you contribute much to the conservation of our world's natural resources. While it may seem to some folks that hunters are destroyers of nature, the truth is that by helping control the numbers of animals that consume resources such as grasses and trees, hunters help maintain productive land that can support wildlife, keep game populations healthy by controlling overpopulation, and contribute to conservation efforts through fees.

Be committed to a wounded animal. A hunter who exhausts all of his available knowledge, energy, and time tracking and finding an animal that has suffered a near-fatal shot is to be respected. People who hunt and don't give their very best effort to recovery don't deserve to be called hunters.

Don't forget to thank the Creator of the outdoors for giving you such wonderful places and experiences to enjoy.

Wanting your neighbor's land, his gear, his gun, his bow, his trophies, his vehicles, and especially his wife who loves hunting is flat out wrong and will cause great frustration. And saying, "I don't want his...I just want some exactly like it" doesn't really work either. That's "coveting in camo."

As tempting as it is, don't hunt while driving. I've been guilty of this…to the detriment of my vehicle. When driving, using your eyes for anything other than monitoring the road and traffic around you may seriously wound your expensive sheet metal.

Don't be surprised or dismayed by a waning desire to hunt in your later years or be critical of young hunters who seem to be a bit bloodthirsty. Both of these extremes are naturally occurring stages in the normal course of a hunter's life.

Honor the setting aside of a day for the Lord. A day of rest is good for the hunter and the hunted. Leaving the woods and the things that live in it for a day allows nature to settle down. Overhunting tampers with the quality of the "fair chase." As for the hunter's need to rest, God designed people like people designed car batteries. We need to recharge.

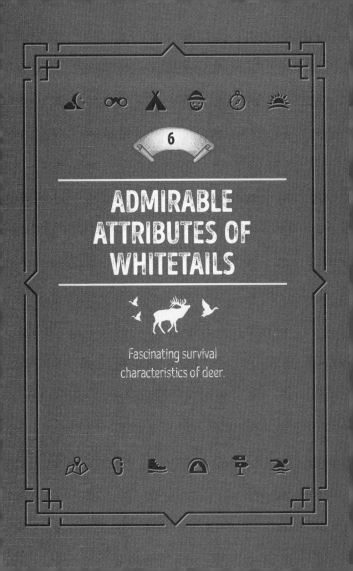

6

ADMIRABLE ATTRIBUTES OF WHITETAILS

Fascinating survival
characteristics of deer.

A whitetail fawn has at least three natural defenses:

- It's extremely difficult for a coyote to detect its smell.

- More than 300 spots on the fawn's coat help it blend into the shadows caused by sunlight filtering through the trees and high weeds.

- The glands between the points of its hooves don't secrete the waxy deposit common to older deer until it's developed running skills. This makes it difficult for predators to track it.

T he brilliantly colored white fur on the underside of the whitetail's tail is often used to signal or "flag" other deer that danger is present. Some believe deer also use their raised white tails to startle pursuing predators. The sight of white tails "bouncing" into a thicket signals to hunters that they've been outsmarted by deer once again.

The sharp, whistlelike sound a deer makes through its nose alerts its comrades of im-pending danger. A deer also makes this noise to startle enemies and give it time to get away. The unexpected loud snort of an undetected deer will test the cardiac condition of hunters every time.

The sharp, hard hooves of deer can inflict great harm to an enemy. By leaping and pouncing, the whitetail can mortally wound poisonous snakes. Whitetails have been known to stand on their back legs and fight with their front hooves—a boxing match every hunter should avoid.

Because a deer's eyes are set high and wide on its head, it can see almost all the way around itself. When its head is down and feeding, movement in any direction except directly behind it is detectable.

A deer's eye has the unusual capability of simultaneously focusing on both near and faraway objects. This ability severely limits the deer's depth perception—a great advantage for hunters.

The deep cupping at the base of a deer's ear creates a sound trap, effectively increasing the deer's hearing. Along with that, the ears' width and height and ability to rotate approximately 300 degrees gives the animal great protection.

The nose of the whitetail is nearly unmatched in the animal kingdom. The olfactory system is made up of thousands of glands that can detect even the faintest airborne odors.

Some hunters contend whitetails have a "sixth sense" that enables them to know danger is in their area. There is no proof of this, but my presence has been detected by deer plenty of times when I thought there was no way it could happen. My theory is that this "sixth sense" is more likely a product of one of the six tattletales I take with me to the woods: body smell, breath odor, aromas trapped in clothing, noise, color and contrast in clothing, and movement.

7

WHEN THINGS
GO WRONG

Reasons for missed
shots and blunders
(and what they really mean).

The gun wouldn't fire. (I forgot to load it.)

I had a problem with my gun rest. (Jack sneezed the moment I pulled the trigger and made the truck shake.)

The ducks just weren't cooperating today. (I couldn't hit the broad side of a barn with a shotgun even if I were standing inside.)

I didn't see a thing this morning. (I was sound asleep.)

I ran out of light and couldn't take the shot. (The truck battery died.)

I got lost while in the mountains but managed to find my way back. (I can't read a compass, and the helicopter ride was really fun.)

The deer came in under me and stood broadside at 12 yards. It was a nice one, but I decided to be merciful and let it walk. (I was eating a candy bar and opening a bottle of pop when the critter appeared.)

The deer spooked and took off. (Because of a severe case of buck fever, my arm muscles suddenly froze up and the string felt as taut as a piano wire. The excited shaking of the rest of my body resulted in the arrow bouncing out of the rest and clattering to the ground.)

I had the crosshairs right on that bull, but the scope must have gotten knocked out of alignment. (I haven't shot this rifle in two years and didn't take the time to sight it in.)

∞

But officer, I didn't know I was on posted property. (I avoided asking the farmer so I could say what I'm saying right now and not feel so guilty.)

📷

That gobbler saw me move and took off like a rocket. (I have the patience of a toddler.)

If I could've stayed out five more minutes I'd have nailed that old buck. (I've messed up enough times before today to know my wife would shoot me if I didn't get home on time.)

I was coming to full draw on a gigantic buck when a sudden weird noise blew the shot. (I've never figured out how to set that stupid cell phone to vibrate mode.)

The huge bear appeared about 10 yards from me, looked right at me, and then bolted back into the woods. (I screamed like a kid on a playground and threw my rifle at him.)

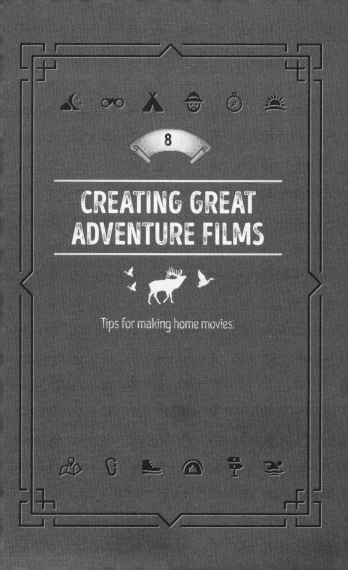

8

CREATING GREAT ADVENTURE FILMS

Tips for making home movies.

U*se discretion.* Some folks who see your film may not be hunters. Graphic scenes of blood spurting, entrails oozing, animals writhing in pain or dying should be avoided. The film should look like a hunt, not a torture, murder, or execution scene.

S howing excited emotion after successfully outsmarting a wary animal is great footage. But don't overlook the fact that jubilant displays such as high-fives and arm pumps after taking the life of an animal could be misunderstood as celebrating the kill instead of acknowledging the skill used to meet the challenge of hunting. One time I had to explain what came across as too much exuberance on film to some non-hunters. It wasn't pleasant. So I urge you to do what I do now—exercise reasonable restraint when it's time to savor a successful hunt.

When being filmed kneeling over a deceased animal, *consider your words carefully*. Certain words can confuse some who are watching. If you say "beautiful," for example, viewers might comment, "If the animal was so beautiful, why did you kill it?" To avoid problems, use words or phrases such as "Huge!" "What a rack!" "Look at this trophy!" One of my favorite choices is "Dinner!"

Foul language should always be avoided. This is especially true when filming. Not only does it sound unintelligent, offensive language means your hunting film may not be appropriate for your children, grandkids, preacher, or conservative in-laws. It would be a shame to not show the footage to everyone…right?

N*ever shoot an animal for the sake of recording a kill.* This shows blatant disrespect for the life of the creature. The purpose of documenting your hunt is to record memories to keep and share, not to show off your skills, prove your manhood, or any other self-centered reason.

K*now your camera.* Whether filming someone or being filmed, the person holding the camera should be familiar with operating it. Read the owner's manual closely to learn the important features on the camera and how to access them. If you don't, you risk missing an opportunity that may never come again. I bought a camera to mount to my compound bow. It sits where the stabilizer bar is normally located and doesn't interfere with the flight of arrows. The sun was setting, but there was still enough legal shooting light when a nice 8-point walked in front of my stand. I turned the camera on and filmed the shot. The shadows cast by the trees resulted in limited light and the film turned out dark and grainy. Upon reading the manual I discovered the camera had a "low light" setting that would have opened the lens to bring in more light.

T he pause button. Practice turning your camera on and making sure everything is working. Make sure it's not on pause or just on. One morning I arrowed a really nice buck at 10 yards while sitting in a ground blind. I filmed the entire hunt and was excited about watching it. After I recovered the deer and had time to watch the movie I discovered I'd only turned the camera on. I forgot to push record! If I'd reviewed the process of turning the camera on and going to "record" mode, I would have a great film today.

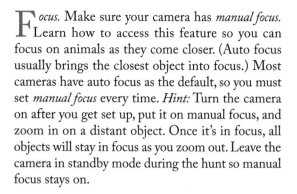

F ocus. Make sure your camera has *manual focus.* Learn how to access this feature so you can focus on animals as they come closer. (Auto focus usually brings the closest object into focus.) Most cameras have auto focus as the default, so you must set *manual focus* every time. *Hint:* Turn the camera on after you get set up, put it on manual focus, and zoom in on a distant object. Once it's in focus, all objects will stay in focus as you zoom out. Leave the camera in standby mode during the hunt so manual focus stays on.

*H*ave *extra batteries and memory sources.* Always carry extra film or memory disks in your pack. Invest in extra batteries so you never face the dreadful "low battery" light when a big buck shows up.

*D*ocument *successes and failures.* Recording successes in the woods is always exciting, but don't forget missed shots, wrong decisions, animals that get away, and other scenes that reveal the challenges of hunting. Revealing the truth that emotions while hunting run the gamut from elation to despair makes good contrast and will contribute to the quality and interest of your story.

Before turning on the camera *think of your story line.* If your film is "A Day in the Life of Dad, the Mighty Hunter," you'll want to show what happens from before daylight all the way to the hunt's end and your trip home.

If you have plenty of memory, *film some "B" roll footage: the scenery, small critters* that enter your area, *parts of the drive* to the hunting spot, *and other scenes.* These will add color and interesting transitions to your scenes.

An *outboard microphone* is a great investment. If you don't have a wireless mic that can be attached to your camera, make sure your subjects are close enough to be heard.

After you've recorded your kill, give some thought to what you'll say before filming the "afterglow." You can even write down what you want to say and use it as a sort of teleprompter. *Avoid retelling the story.* The viewer just watched it. Tell what you learned from the hunt, share what you're feeling, and give insights the camera may not have picked up on.

Make sure your "time and date" stamp feature is *turned off* while you film. The numbers are very annoying while viewing and get in the way of adding interesting titles to scenes.

Add *descriptive titles and captions* to your film. Be creative and incorporate humor into your choices. Also put your name, the date, and the location someplace on the film so later generations will know who you are and where you were.

9

HUNTING IFS

When you need a reality check.

If a wild turkey's incredible eyesight were accompanied by a sense of smell as good as a deer or bear's, most turkey tags would never be filled.

If you must depart the woods at 9:30 AM to keep in your spouse's good favor, you'll hear leaves crunching behind your stand at 9:28…or 9:29.

If your mate says "Have fun!" as you're heading out, you can rest assured you're doing something right. If your spouse says, "May the gnats of a thousand hot summers infest your ears today," you can be sure you're doing something really wrong.

If you're single and love to hunt and you meet a woman who has a picture of her latest whitetail as a screensaver on her computer or cell phone, seriously consider matrimony.

If you're a dedicated hunter and getting married, carefully avoid setting the wedding date on or near hunting seasons. Be generous in your margins. Don't set a date that may even come close to possible season openers.

If a deer crosses in front of you on the highway, don't watch it. Instead, look behind it. Other deer are probably following the leader.

If a bear had the eyesight of a turkey and the ears of a deer, many bear tags would remain unpunched.

If you set up a stand on the north side of a field, deer will enter on the south side. If you move the stand to that location the following day, the deer will enter the field on the north side. If you compromise on the third day and set up your stand in the middle, they'll enter on the north and south sides. That's why it's called "hunting."

If "shooting light" ends at 5:56, deer will appear at 5:58. Don't push the envelope and take a shot. The low light will hinder a sure shot, and darkness makes tracking and finding a wounded deer extremely difficult. To avoid temptation, establish your "don't shoot in the twilight" standard before you head out for the hunt.

If a bird lands on your rifle, shotgun, or bow while deer hunting, it's a sure sign that the biggest buck you've ever seen is about to walk by…but you won't be awake to see it.

If you're sitting on the ground during a warm spring day during gobbler season and a snake crawls up your pant leg, its okay to dance and scream. Just don't shoot!

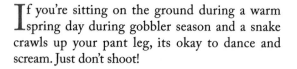

If you come into contact with poison ivy while hunting, you have my sympathy.

If you have to choose between buying a new lawn mower or a new rifle, you have way too much yard.

If your anniversary falls on opening day of deer season, do the right thing and try to be home by noon.

If you can't fall asleep the night before a hunt, try counting all the things you should be doing the next day besides hunting.

If you hear the explosive report of a rifle, you're supposedly safe because bullets travel faster than sound. I'm not sure, but I think that's a comforting thought.

If you need to leave the office at one o'clock so you can settle into your deer stand by three, turn your phone off at 12:45.

If you get to your hunting area and someone is already there, quietly apologize, slip away very slowly, and fight the intense urge to break into an operatic, boisterous version of "The hills are alive with the sound of music!" in an effort to discourage the other hunter.

If the new guy at deer camp warns you he snores loudly and might keep you up all night, pat him gently on the jaw at bedtime and say, "That's okay. I'll be right here beside you if you need me." You'll likely get all the sleep you need.

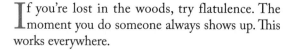

If you're lost in the woods, try flatulence. The moment you do someone always shows up. This works everywhere.

If you come home from a hunt and your nonhunter spouse asks, "Did you see anything today?" keep in mind it's probably one of the few times she'll be fully satisfied with a one word answer.

If a landowner allows you to hunt on his property, be a good sportsman and offer to help with a chore or task. If he says that's not necessary, wait 10 seconds and offer again.

If you pull the trigger of your muzzle-loader and it doesn't fire, *do not* lower it from your shoulder immediately. The charge may just be delayed. Wait several seconds while pointing the barrel to the ground. Getting sucker punched by an unexpected discharge of a "smoke pole" is painful.

If the animal you're pursuing is standing on the other side of a fence—on property you don't have permission to hunt—don't shoot. Venison seasoned with guilt is never tasty.

If you want 100-percent accuracy when shooting, practice 200 percent.

If it's buck-only season and you catch sight of a deer heading your way but it's too far away to discern gender, it's okay to pray for antlers.

If you need to put oil on a moving part of your bow or gun for smoother operation or to prevent rust, use a natural oil such as canola, olive, or peanut. Petroleum-based oil has an odor that may put deer on alert.

If you use a portable treestand that uses cloth on its seat, during the off-season store the stand in a place without unwanted odors. Garages and outbuildings where lawn mowers or tractors are parked may result in the cloth absorbing the smell of gasoline. If you must store a stand in a building where unnatural odors are present, enclose the stand in a large, sealed plastic bag filled with tree leaves.

If you need toilet paper and someone suggests using a dollar, don't use small change.

If you're an Easterner flying out West to hunt or vice versa, arrive a day earlier than necessary to avoid the potential trauma of airport delays due to weather or mechanical failure.

If you want to know who your very best friend is, the answer is who you call on your cell after you just got *the* big one.

If you use a wristwatch that has an alarm feature or have a watch that beeps hourly, make sure these settings are off when you get to your hunting area…unless your marriage or job depends on you being reminded of an important departure time.

If you take a still picture of your kill, avoid showing entry or exit wounds, oozing blood or froth, a hanging tongue, or any other image that might be offensive to nonhunters.

If you find a licking branch that is six feet off the ground, a scrape that is four feet or more in diameter, and a rub on a tree with a trunk more than six inches wide, you've located a sizable buck. *Do not put your stand in that area.* I'm on my way!

10

UNIQUE ANIMAL
FACTS

Interesting features
God gave creatures.

Hare and Rabbits. The most obvious differences between a hare and a rabbit are the ears and legs. The hare's are much longer compared to its body size. At birth the distinctions between the two are even more profound. Baby hare are born with fur and their eyes are open. They can walk and hop within hours of birth. Rabbits are born naked, blind, and helpless. A young hare is called a "leveret," French for "first year." Baby rabbits are called kits or kittens.

Bison. Male and female bison have permanent horns. When the Plains Indians killed a bison, they used nearly every part of the body: meat for food, sinew for binding an arrow to a shaft, bones for making bows, tallow for waterproofing, hides for clothing and shelter, bile for creating yellow paint, hooves for making glue, long hair for braiding rope, tails for fly swatters, dung for fuel, and internal organs for containers.

Ring-necked pheasants. These game birds thrive in fields across much of the United States. Weighing in at nearly 3 pounds, the males are spectacularly and iridescently colored. They have a red face patch, brilliant green head, and white ring on the neck (usually). Their bodies are patterned in soft brown and russet, and they have long, barred tail feathers. Females are slightly smaller with mottled light brown heads and bodies. Introduced in the U.S. in the mid to late 1800s, part of the ring-necked pheasant population started when 28 or 30 Chinese pheasants were shipped by the U.S. Consul General at Shanghai to Oregon's Willamette Valley. Other shipments soon followed.

Wild turkeys. The largest game bird in North America, the turkey can weigh as much as 26 pounds. It reaches maturity at 2 years and lives approximately 9. Male turkeys have a "pectoral tuft," more commonly known as its beard. This growth of feathers on its head is horsetail-like in appearance. Although more common to males, known as toms, females (hens) do grow them occasionally. A bearded female is usually a bit more aggressive than other females and is regarded with respect among the ladies.

R*uffed grouse*. "Ruffed grouse" comes from the Latin and Greek words *umbellus bonasa*. *Umbellus* refers to the umbrellalike ruffs of dark feathers located on the neck of the bird. *Bonasa* means "a bison" and refers to the bird's drumming noise that resembles the sound of bellowing buffalo. Contrary to common belief, the drumming sound is not created by the bird striking its body or the log it usually sits on when drumming. The noise is generated by the bird's wings beating the air in a circular motion. The sound is essentially a miniature sonic boom.

B*ighorn sheep*. One of the most amazing assets of the surefooted bighorn is its very strong, cushioned feet. Each foot has two rubberlike pads that enable the critter to hold on to nearly any surface whether wet, dry, smooth, sharp, soft, or hard. Along with its padded feet are sharp dew claws on its legs that can be used as brakes. By either bending or straightening its powerful legs, these brakes can be applied to manage the rate of descent as it leaps and lands. Bighorns have excellent eyesight, and it's almost impossible to approach them without being detected.

P *rairie dogs.* Small rodents in the squirrel family, prairie dogs live in a network of burrows commonly called "towns" that are divided into wards. Each ward is subdivided into family groups called "coteries." Natural ground features, such as hills and streams, are used as boundaries. If two prairie dogs meet at one of these boundaries, they lower their heads and gently rub lips. They rub on one side and then the other to smell each other and identify relatives. If one determines the other is not family, a fight ensues. Considered a pest for many years, the prairie dog is now starting to get respect as a vital part of prairie ecosystems.

R *ed squirrels.* As a red squirrel balances on a branch in preparation to leap, it lifts its head several times to compare the angle of sight between where it is and where it's going. This "nodding" helps the squirrel correctly gauge the distance so it can jump safely across the expanse. The scientific term for this process is "parallax."

*E*agles. Baby eagles, called eaglets, typically fly between their tenth and fifteenth week. If a young bird is hesitant, the parents will leave food on a nearby branch to entice the young bird out of the nest. (A great idea for human parents if their grown child tends to stay too long.)

*B*luebirds. When a young bluebird discharges excreta, it is wrapped neatly in a small durable sack. The parent carries it away and the nest remains unsoiled. (Why didn't God create human babies with this feature?)

*M*onarch butterflies. The first meal of the monarch butterfly caterpillar is its own egg shell. When that is finished, it turns to the nearest leaf of the milkweed where it was hatched. The amount of milkweed consumed within two weeks is so much that the size of the caterpillar is increased 2,700 times. If a human baby did the same thing, it would grow from an average of 6 pounds at birth to over 8 tons!

Grizzly bears. Most people assume grizzlies consume massive amounts of food just before hibernation. However, bears actually fast just prior to entering winter rest. This makes their stomachs and intestines clean and empty for hibernation. During hibernation bears require very little energy because their systems slow down.

Crows. To gather a "murder" of crows to a specific area, use an owl decoy. Owls are the crow's most dreaded foe. To keep this bird of prey out of their territory, crows mass together to dive bomb the unwelcome intruder and create such a racket that the noise-sensitive owl withdraws.

Wood ducks. These ducks understand the danger of educating predators about the whereabouts of their nest. To avoid revealing its location they seldom fly there directly. Instead they approach from different directions and then perch in a nearby tree, carefully watching to see if predators are in the area. If none are present, they fly to the nest.

Skunks. Skunks are typically friendly creatures and won't use their legendary scent defense unless provoked. When a skunk does feel it's necessary to spray, it quickly looks the attacker in the eye and instantly swings its body around. With its tail raised (a sure sign of an impending "stink shower"), a tube protrudes that is aimed at the enemy's eye. A skunk's pinpoint accuracy has been measured up to 16 feet.

Woodchucks. Commonly known as groundhogs, these large rodents like to build homes with hidden escape routes. When a fox or other predator nears, a woodchuck hurries to the main entrance of his den and stands watch. If the fox chooses to pursue the critter, the woodchuck ducks into the den and escapes through the well-concealed, carefully constructed exit.

B*eavers.* These large rodents can remain underwater for an amazing 17 minutes thanks to extra-large lungs and an oversized liver (stores oxygenated blood). Phenomenal den builders, beavers log trees with their strong teeth and create dams across creeks and streams to form ponds so their homes are partially submerged, giving them protection from predators.

C*hipmunks.* The chipmunk's name, *Tamias,* means "one who lays up or stores." This worthy description of the smallest of the squirrel family features its industrious nature. As a chipmunk prepares for winter, it tirelessly works from dawn to dusk to find and warehouse food. A chipmunk can gather and store as much as a bushel of food in a three-day period. Its ability to carry massive quantities of food in its cheek pouches is impressive. One chipmunk's "shopping trip" could be 13 prune stones or 31 corn kernels or 32 beechnuts or 65 sunflower seeds or 145 grains of wheat.

Foxes. When humans are afraid or experience other strong, negative emotions, our bodies emit an odor undetectable by us but picked up by a fox's excellent olfactory system. These aromas give the fox distinct messages. If fear is detected, a fox is more apt to be aggressive and hold its ground. If it senses confidence, the fox will likely retreat.

Bobcats. One thing that causes a bobcat the most trouble is its insatiable curiosity. Almost everything that attracts its attention will be checked out. Old-time trappers used this overly investigative nature to their advantage. Many bobcats were caught in traps baited with a little bit of catnip oil. Bobcats are very shy and won't approach humans. They don't make good pets.

11

HUNTING HUMOR

Conversation starters for
driving to and from hunts.

What does fried rattlesnake taste like?

A really long chicken.

What is the key to making a 500-yard shot with my rifle?

Move 300 yards closer.

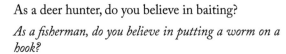

As a deer hunter, do you believe in baiting?

As a fisherman, do you believe in putting a worm on a hook?

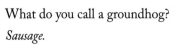

That deer is really torn up. What weapon did you use?

A Chevy .06.

What do you call a groundhog?

Sausage.

In sports, highly successful moments have names like slam-dunk, home run, hole-in-one, and touchdown. What do you call a great archery shot?

Food.

How do I quarter an elk if I get one and I'm hunting alone?

Nickel and dime it instead.

How are grizzly bear hunting and flying an airplane similar?

Both involve hours of waiting interrupted by moments of intense fear.

What did you learn from the buck you bagged during rut season?

If you chase women you might get shot!

In states such as Montana, Colorado, and Oregon, antler points on a deer are counted by saying "six by six," "seven by seven," or just a "six point." What do Easterners call a similar-sized deer in their area?

A coronary maker.

Is there a culinary name for "road kill" deer?

Grilled venison.

"Can you go huntin' with me this weekend?"

"Sure! I can hunt anytime I want."

Later to spouse: "Honey, do I want to go huntin' today?"

If a deer had no eyes what would it be called?

I have no-eye-deer!

What do you call a hunter who goes the entire season without getting a deer?

A vegetarian.

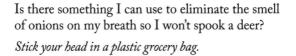

If a tree falls in the woods and no one is around to hear it, will it still make noise?

Was a deer hunter in it?

If there something I can use to eliminate the smell of onions on my breath so I won't spook a deer?

Stick your head in a plastic grocery bag.

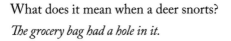

What does it mean when a deer snorts?

The grocery bag had a hole in it.

What does a deer grunt sound like?

Beans.

"I'd like to hunt deer in a new and unusual way. Any suggestions?"

"Unique up on it."

What is the key to tracking and finding an arrowed deer?

A perfectly placed shot.

What do you call twin fawns before they're born?

Womb mates.

How can I transfer the patience I have on a deer stand to my life as a husband and father?

By carefully reconsidering your understanding of the word "trophy."

KNOWING NOSES

How to avoid smelling like a human.

One of the greatest challenges for the archery hunter is that the shooting distance of an arrow is seriously less than a bullet fired from a gun. Perhaps the most formidable obstacle for some types of hunts is the efficiency of the olfactory systems of animals such as bear, deer, and elk. I've heard the comparison that a deer can smell and differentiate odors the way we see colors. For that reason human scent suppression is essential. Though a hunter can't completely eliminate his odor footprint, there are ways to successfully outsmart an animal's nose.

Anything that smells the least bit out of the ordinary immediately alerts an animal. So study where you'll be hunting. Determine what plants, fruit, soil, and other natural odor producers are common to the area. In Tennessee black walnuts are plentiful, and the odor of the nut is unique and strong. During the early part of the season I carry three or four with me when I hunt. When I settle into a treestand, I crack the shell, letting the pieces fall to the ground to mask my human scent. (The juice in the green shells of unripe black walnuts stains skin yellow. Use gloves!)

Make use of odors common to your hunting area. Tobacco farming is huge in my area and much of the tobacco is "dark fired" (cured) in barns. The smoking process usually runs from mid to late August through October. After realizing the deer in my area were accustomed to tobacco smoke, I asked a neighbor to let me store my camo clothes in one of his barns. He permitted it, and later that year, when I went to the woods, I smelled like a smoking barn. I'll never forget that morning! I mounted a ladder stand at a field edge. The wind was blowing behind me toward the field, directly at a mature buck that entered within arrow range. It never knew I was there! I shot the deer at 12 yards, and it's the biggest deer I've ever taken in terms of points—16 by Eastern standards.

Bathe with scent-free soap and shampoo. Use scent-free deodorant.

Set aside a few towels for drying off after a shower during hunting season. Wash them in scent-free detergent and let them air dry. Putting a towel in a dryer is a mistake due to the residual odors left by fabric softener sheets.

Wash your hunting clothes (including underwear and socks) with scent-free detergent and let them air dry. After they're thoroughly dry, "marinate" them in plastic bags partially filled with leaves from trees in your hunting area. In my area I use dried oak leaves.

Because human breath can be saturated with odors, avoid foods with pungent smells, such as onions or garlic, the night before a hunt. Brush your teeth before you head to the woods. In addition, sweeten your breath often while on the stand. I usually take an apple and bite into it every few minutes. I let it soak in my mouth rather than chew it. The smell of apples on my breath helps color the air that will eventually find an animal's nose. Peanuts are a good alternative to apples. Also, fruit-flavored hard candies, such as Jolly Rancher Green Apple, yield good cover.

One of the smartest things God did when He designed the human body was to put the nose as far as possible from the feet. Sour feet and smelly boots can be a hunt killer. If your feet or boots smell awful, you will probably save on ammo costs.

Avoid stopping at convenience stores on the way to the hunt. If you do stop, the likely result is hair and clothes that smell like burnt coffee, biscuits and gravy, overcooked corndogs, and an ashtray.

Dress for the hunt at your vehicle. Keep your camo in the plastic bags filled with dried foliage until you get to the hunting site so they won't absorb any vehicle odors.

Hunt above the animal's nose if possible. A stand high enough to allow your scent to pass above a deer gives you a distinct advantage.

Carry a large plastic bag and an extra T-shirt in your pack. If it's hot out and you sweat through an undershirt, remove it, place it in the plastic bag, and seal it. Put on the clean shirt. This little step will keep your human scent at a minimum, and a dry T-shirt will be warmer as the temperature wanes during the day.

Don't spit when hunting. Human saliva has distinct odors that linger. If you have to spit, use a jar with a lid.

Work the wind. Even if you reduce your human scent to one percent, if the wind flows over your back and toward an animal's nose, the critter will likely be on guard. Keep the wind in your face whenever possible.

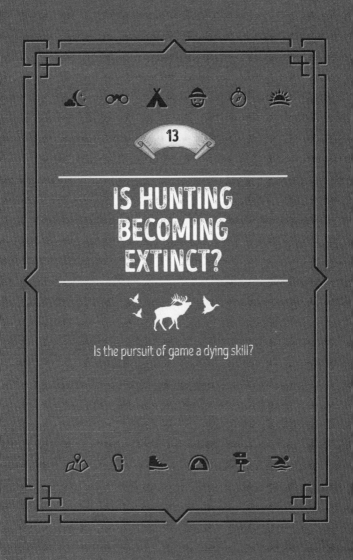

13

IS HUNTING BECOMING EXTINCT?

Is the pursuit of game a dying skill?

In *Whitetail: Rites of Autumn,* Charles Alsheimer notes that "a by-product of society's shift from an agrarian to an urban setting has been a decline in the number of deer hunters entering the woods each fall." Here are some reasons he gives and my insights in italics.

1. Dysfunctional families. *If moms and dads become single parents through divorce or separation, both parents often must enter the workplace. The time available for outdoor activities is drastically reduced. And, if not monitored carefully, hunting can interfere with family time, especially when children need their parents' undivided attention.*

2. Peer pressure. *Opposition to citizens owning firearms is growing as people equate the escalating violence in society with the availability of guns. Peer pressure may keep some hunters out of the woods, especially if they feel their social acceptance is in jeopardy.*

3. Competing activities. *So many activities vie for our time that hunting may get lost in the shuffle. From making a living*

(or a killing in some cases) to playing, from managing technology (computers) to social events, from exercising to waiting motionless on clogged freeways, finding time for forays into the woods can be difficult.

4. Poor recruitment of hunters. *Although stores that sell hunting gear do a great job making the outdoors look attractive, the number of new hunters is declining. One major contributor is there are few organizations that promote hunting to the public. Another problem is the public relations disasters caused by the uncouth behavior of some hunters, including the dangerous combination of alcohol and guns, the displaying of kills without discretion, and trespassing. Another lack is mature hunters who are willing to mentor young hunters and include them on hunting trips.*

5. Lack of places to hunt. *With new home construction, city expansion, and industry consuming large tracts of land, it's harder to secure a place to hunt. That's the result of progress, but it sure creates a dilemma for hunters.*

Besides showing good ethics as a hunter, Charles notes one way to reverse the trend of a diminishing hunting population:

The average age of the [deer] hunter in America is now 46 years, up nearly 10 years from a decade ago. Without the recruitment of younger hunters, it will be difficult to attain the deer harvest required to keep whitetail herds in line with the range's carrying capacity. It involves taking a kid to the woods at an early age on a repeated basis.

I fully agree with this suggestion and encourage you to check out chapter 15, "Getting Your Kids Interested in Hunting."

The Five Stages of a Deer Hunter

Adapted from *Whitetail Strategies*
by Charles Alsheimer

1. *The Shooter Stage* occurs when the hunter learns he can't get enough of hunting and shooting. Feeling successful and experiencing accomplishment is important.*

2. *The Limiting Out Stage.* The goal is to harvest as many animals as legally permissible.

3. *The Trophy Stage.* Hunter has enough knowledge of his quarry that he can be selective. Bigger antlers and a keen knowledge of stewarding the whitetail resource takes center stage in the hunter's life.

4. *The Method Stage.* The hunter is mellowing. With many autumns under his belt, his interest turns more toward how the hunt is done. Often the hunter will move from weapon to weapon for the challenge the differences provide. Understanding deer behavior also becomes paramount.

5. *The Sportsman's Stage.* The hunter has a deeper understanding of why being a hunter is meaningful. Because he knows deer behavior very well and has prob-

* Moving to the next stage doesn't mean the previous stage is abandoned.

ably harvested many, he turns to aspects of "legacy building." He may become involved in the preservation of hunting and make a conscious effort to see that the joy of hunting is passed on to the next generation. Many hunters acquire property to hunt on.

14

HUNTING YOUR MATE'S FAVOR

Surefire ways to help your spouse
not hate what you love to do.

One of the greatest thrills of being out in creation is encountering the awesomeness of the Creator. If you've looked up to the sky in the darkness of predawn and seen a massive expanse of stars that made you whisper, "Way to go, God!" you know what I'm talking about. When this kind of rendezvous with God's greatness happens, tell your spouse about it. She'll realize you're getting more out of the hunting experience than just an opportunity to feed your addiction to the excitement of the pursuit.

Be fair with family funds. Investing money in your hobby and not being willing to do the same for your spouse's is a huge mistake. One idea that has worked wonders in my marriage is "the equal cash method." If I spend $20 on a hunting item, I give my wife, Annie, the same amount in cash. This lets her know I want to be fair in handling our money and that I treasure our relationship. Try it with your mate!

Make sure your fun isn't your spouse's fear. Guns, bullets, razor-sharp broadheads, tree-stands, snakes, bears, and a host of other exciting-but-dangerous elements await the hunter. Assure your mate you're careful. Demonstrate how knowledgeable you are about your weapon and safety. Tell her how careful you are when placing and climbing into a treestand. Let her see you check your gear for flaws. I even take my cell phone along, to Annie's great comfort. (But remember to put it on vibrate when you're on the hunt!) Your willingness to recognize your mate's concerns and do something about them will garner you many points.

Don't let your leisure become your mate's labor. If your spouse has to clean up after you, her appreciation for your hobby will wane in a serious way. Some of the complaints I've heard from wives about their husbands' post-hunt habits include mud strewn throughout the house from dirty boots, blood on clothes and carpet, carcass remnants in the yard, and uncontrolled, dirty dogs that create havoc inside and outside. Next time you come home from a hunt, take time to notice what you're doing…and if changes are necessary—make them.

Don't mess with traditions. Unless going hunting is mutually agreed upon in advance of special days traditionally reserved for family activities, don't go. Holidays, weddings, anniversaries, and birthdays aren't the best days to announce you're going hunting. Keeping in your family's good will—especially your spouse's—is a monumental trophy.

Involve your children in your love of the outdoors. Take them along on hunts! You'll accomplish two great things. First, the parent who stays behind gets a needed break from the rigors of childcare. When I took our kids on adventures, Annie always looked so refreshed when we returned. She really appreciated my effort to give her a few hours of alone time. Second, the time my kids and I spent together "out there" helped build strong relationships between us.

When something happens in the animal kingdom or in nature that improves your character, let your spouse know. Perhaps the most obvious example of this relates to deer. A buck makes himself vulnerable to a hunter's aim when he throws his usual cautiousness to the wind during rut and chases does. This "buck gone crazy" scenario is a reminder to us not to be foolish and forsake moral alertness. Your mate will appreciate this insight and the accompanying declaration of your fidelity.

Don't give your spouse "clouds and wind without the rain." Proverbs 25:14 reveals how disappointed a farmer is when his dry and thirsty land is teased by clouds and wind that suddenly appear but then pass without delivering rain. When you tell your mate you'll be home at ten o'clock, make every effort to keep that promise. If you don't, she'll be very disappointed. And if you break your word often, even if it's unintentional, she'll soon resent and resist your hunting excursions.

Turn your passion into a mission. Use your knowledge and skills to mentor youngsters in how to hunt safely. When they have the knowledge down, go the extra mile and take them to the woods or meadows or ponds. You can also guide handicapped hunters to game, feed the hungry with meat garnered from a hunt, and organize events designed to expand spiritual awareness and hunting knowledge for fellow hunters.

If a taxidermist has turned your trophies into works of art, don't assume your spouse will want them in the living room. A smart husband will let his mate decide where hunting memorabilia goes. Never forget she views home as a nest, and she's probably the one more vested in its decor. "Buck up and doe the right thing!" And if your wife loves taxidermy, count your blessings and get out the nails and stud finder.

From personal experience I can vouch that Annie is really pleased when I keep my hunting gear out of sight…and in another building. She's mentioned more than once the messes we've seen in homes where hunters leave camo, boots, hats, gloves, equipment, and mud throughout the house. If you don't have an outbuilding, invest in a large storage bin and consolidate your stuff into one place. Make sure the place is secure and dry.

Show genuine interest in your mate's hobbies. Investing time, resources, and energy in what your spouse likes to do is a great way to gain and maintain a healthy balance between your own hobby and your marriage. Be willing to share in her hobby once in a while. As far as I know, no man has died from shopping or gardening with his wife.

15

GETTING
YOUR KIDS
INTERESTED
IN HUNTING

How to encourage your
children in the outdoors.

*C*losely monitor your child's emotions. This is especially critical during the initial hunting experiences. If your child is distressed at the life of an animal (regardless of size) being taken, don't ignore the troubled feelings. Explain that taking an animal's life is a solemn event and emphasize the aspects of the hunt that justify the death, such as using the meat for sustenance. Be sensitive to the possibility that hunting may not suit your child.

*D*on't force kids to stay outside in terrible weather. Extreme temperatures are difficult to endure as an adult, much less as a child. Excessive sweating in the heat or uncontrollable trembling in the bitter cold are sure signs it's time to pack up and head home. Keep the hunting experience positive.

P ractice is fun. Veteran hunters may have forgotten how much enjoyment shooting a gun or bow is for younger folks. Making things go boom and poking holes in a target can be pure delight for youngsters. Make practice time enjoyable and promote the challenge of making good, consistent shots. An ongoing, *friendly* competition—along with incentives for winning the contests (such as a nominal dollar amount, new equipment, gift cards, promised hunts)—can keep a child practicing. The ultimate benefit is increasing your child's confidence so the actual hunt will be successful and positive.

S tart small. One of the best critters for a first-timer to hunt is the squirrel. In most areas of the country bushytails are plentiful and provide plenty of action. (Rabbits are considered small game, but their quickness may discourage new hunters). Also, the caliber of gun needed for small game is either a .410 shotgun that has a mild kick or a shoulder friendly .22 rifle.

Use a tent blind. One of the best items of equipment hunters with kids can purchase is a pop-up blind. They provide protection from finger-numbing winds in cold weather and skin-melting sunshine in the warmer parts of a season. Blinds also permit freedom of movement for children who have a hard time sitting still. The liberty to stand up as well as communicate often makes waiting for game easier.

Don't do everything for the new hunter. Doing everything for your child except pulling the trigger is a common mistake for many mentors. Make sure the youngster gets to enjoy the challenge of locating deer, setting up stands, working on scent suppression, and understanding weapon handling.

Strategy. One of the most enjoyable parts of hunting with another person is figuring out and planning how to outsmart the wary critters being hunted. Drawing pictures, identifying and naming certain parts of the property to be hunted, studying topographical maps, and developing strategy will pique the interest of a young person and keep his or her mind engaged.

Invest in good clothing and boots. Nothing says "I wanna go home" louder than boots that don't provide enough warmth or comfort for the longest possible amount of time. Gloves, socks, and under-garments that are too thin are deal breakers when it comes to enjoying being outdoors. Spending the extra cash on high-quality clothing can mean the difference between "I want to go hunting with you!" and "Don't make me do that again!"

*D*ocument the memories. Besides the enjoyment and treasure that having a hunt documented provides, the technology and logistics involved in filming a hunt can capture the interest of a new hunter. Also, digital cameras are a wonderful addition to a child's day pack. Allowing him or her to snap pictures then download and send them to family and friends will deepen his or her interest in the outdoors. (See the "Creating Great Adventure Films" chapter.)

*I*nstill an appreciation for wildlife in your child's mind and heart. Teach a child to have respect for the life of an animal by showing how to make the quickest, most humane kill possible. Teach the young hunter about conservation and caring for the environment—from not littering to participating in community "clean-up" days.

Teach good hunting ethics. Attend the mandatory Hunter's Safety course with your child. This is good review for you and strengthens your parent/child relationship. Through your words and example let your young hunter understand the importance of honoring all laws. Emphasize ethics even when temptation is high, such as when an animal is just on the other side of a property line. Model respect for other hunters and outdoor enthusiasts, including those who don't advocate hunting.

16

WHEN AN EASTERNER HEADS WEST

One of my dreams was to journey
"out West" to pursue the mighty elk.
Finally I made it...and it fulfilled all my
expectations. I've been back a few times,
and each trip is better than the last. The
following suggestions are not exhaustive,
but they sure made a difference for me.

Block out the date of your hunt at least 18 months in advance. Make sure there isn't a family reunion, wedding, or other momentous event you're expected to attend on your available hunting dates. After you book the hunt and pay the deposit, post your trip on all family calendars so everyone knows you're going. Make sure you mention it every once in a while as a gentle reminder to those you love that you'll be unavailable during your hunting time.

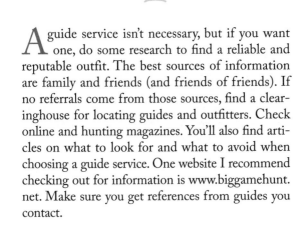

A guide service isn't necessary, but if you want one, do some research to find a reliable and reputable outfit. The best sources of information are family and friends (and friends of friends). If no referrals come from those sources, find a clearinghouse for locating guides and outfitters. Check online and hunting magazines. You'll also find articles on what to look for and what to avoid when choosing a guide service. One website I recommend checking out for information is www.biggamehunt.net. Make sure you get references from guides you contact.

Calculate the amount of cash you'll need to spend on a hunt and then add 15 percent. Travel expenses, out-of-state licenses and fees, and guide service fees are predictable. But there are always costs you don't expect, such as replacing equipment that breaks, delays because of weather, or the need to ship a trophy rack or extra meat home.

Note the deadlines for submitting required applications for licenses for the area you want to hunt. If you use a guide, he or she can be very helpful in making sure you're legally covered for the hunt and provide information such as best times to hunt and transportation needed.

Get in shape. Most Western hunts are in mountainous regions that require extra performance from your leg muscles and will definitely test your lung capacity. Even if your hunt will use horses and pack animals, you won't be on them all the time. Start preparing your body at least six months in advance of the hunt. I vividly remember my first "real" mountain hunt. Even though I'd done extra conditioning, the ascents and descents and even more ascents in the Montana mountains made my Tennessee legs and lungs wonder if they were going to survive.

If you're using a guide, make sure you share any medical conditions or needs you have. If you're disabled in any way, a guide will need to know in advance so he or she can provide the necessary equipment or make the necessary alterations (such as a handicap-accessible cabin).

Practice, practice, practice with your weapons and gear. Nothing can ruin a dream hunt for big game in a Western state like being unprepared. Go to the range several times before departing for the hunt to sight in your gun…and then do it again when you arrive out West. If compound bow hunting, a month before the hunt replace the cables. Then shoot at least 20 shots a day at a distance of 50 yards. If you're using traditional archery equipment, consider the age of the string and replace it if needed. Like a compound bow hunter, you should also be ready for a shot that is longer than you normally like to take.

Have an emergency kit that includes who to contact if you're injured, extra prescriptions or medications you take regularly, medicines for blisters, jock itch, cuts, scrapes, poison oak, and a small repair kit for your weapon.

If you need to ship equipment to the guide service office, use a company that provides a tracking number. Also insure the package. Ship well in advance and mark on the outside with large letters or on a bright label "Hold for (and put your name, date of hunt, phone number, and e-mail address)."

Pack as light as possible. Carrying unnecessary weight up the mountains makes you miserable. (For a humorous look at the hazards of over packing read "The Petrich Method" in my book *A Hunter Sets His Sights*.)

Take plenty of memory sticks/cards and batteries for your camera or camcorder. A small tripod will also be very useful for group shots.

A GPS device is a wonderful option for your pack. If you don't want to spend the extra bucks, a good reliable compass won't hit the wallet hard. Before you go, know how to use all the gear you take.

Take extra batteries for your communication equipment and devices (walkie-talkies, radios, flashlights).

Leave the details of where you plan to hunt (specific sections of a state, geographic locations), guide service contact information, airline flight numbers if appropriate, travel itinerary if driving. Think of anything that will contribute to the comfort level of those who will bid you a temporary farewell, and do your best to provide it.

For the sake of accurately recounting your adventure, I recommend journaling your adventure. Don't worry if writing isn't your thing; just do it. Daily entries regarding the trip out, the hunt, and the trip back will be a treasure for you and also be valued by the hunters behind you on the trail of time. Include your emotions, lessons learned, and other unique aspects of the hunt. This may be handed down through the generations!

17

DEFEATING
POST-SEASON
DOLDRUMS

Surviving and thriving
during the off season

*G*et involved in a sportsman's event such as a wild game dinner. Most organizations wait until a season closes to hold these kinds of functions. If there aren't events near you, start one! Volunteer to help with set up/take down, to cook, or to conduct a seminar based on your specialty as a hunter. The connection to other outdoorsman as you labor beside them yields inspiring fellowship.

*A*ttend a hunting industry expo. Held mostly outside hunting seasons, hunting shows offer exciting looks at new equipment and opportunities to mingle and talk with fellow enthusiasts. With so many equipment makers under one roof, walking the aisles can lead to some very uplifting conversations with experts in the booths as well as friends encountered in the aisles. Plus you might find a good deal that will save you loads of cash if you need to purchase something new or replace something old.

T*ake a youngster to a hunting safety course,* especially a kid you plan to hunt with. Whether the youth is your own offspring or someone else's, his or her life (and yours) can depend on the knowledge and experience gained at these classes. Add to that the joy of passing on the heritage of hunting, and you can quickly chase away the depression of not being able to chase game.

E*njoy your second hobby.* Fishing, motorcycling, photography, bird watching, or team sports can help you while away the time.

*R*ange shooting is a great way to expend some of that energy you can't put into chasing critters. Gathering with others to shoot competitively and/ or for fun brings a little sunshine into the cloudy days of the off-season. You'll also hone your skills as a shooter.

*J*ournal your season of experiences. This is my most favorite thing to do. Not only has it been useful in writing books, but writing my memories of each hunting season gives me a way to pass on my enthusiasm and knowledge to those I love…and even on to future generations. Besides, recounting the season in detail is almost like being there again.

Assist the owner of the land you regularly hunt. Work is a very good way to occupy a pining heart. Whether it's mowing the yard, mending fences, operating a combine, plowing, or cutting fallen timber, make yourself available. It's the right thing to do in exchange for hunting rights and has the added benefit of giving you the chance to scout the area.

∞

Work on an invention. During the season did you think of something that could help you as a hunter? The time off from being in the woods is a great time to follow through with some research and then create a prototype of your idea. One year I had a bowstring get bound up in a bulky coat sleeve during a shot. As a result I missed a huge 12-point buck. During the winter I created a coat with a removable sleeve. I still use it today. And who knows, you might get your invention patented and into production!

18

INSIGHTS FOR LIFE

Hunters and animals in God's Word.

"As the deer pants for the water brooks, so pants my soul for You, O God" (Psalm 42:1).

A wise teacher pointed out to me that there are at least two times when a deer gets excessively thirsty: when it is fleeing from danger and when it's engaged in combat. In a similar way, there are at least two times when the human spirit develops a serious thirst: when running from temptation and when doing battle against evil (2 Timothy 2:22; Ephesians 6:12). The best refreshment is the pure water of love and grace offered by God.

"Rejoice in the wife of your youth. As a loving hind and a graceful doe, let her breasts satisfy you at all times" (Proverbs 5:18-19 NASB).

The doe is a study in gracefulness, tenderness, and hygiene. When your "doe" displays these characteristics, let her know how much you appreciate her.

"My son, if you become surety for your friend, if you have shaken hands in pledge for a stranger, you are snared by the words of your mouth...Deliver yourself like a gazelle from the hand of the hunter" (Proverbs 6:1-2,5).

What profound truth! Never be a cosigner for a debt. If you've already made the commitment, honorably remove yourself from the responsibility as quickly as possible...just like an antelope escaping the presence of a hunter.

* * *

"'Behold, I am going to send for many fishermen,'" declares the LORD, 'and they will fish for them; and afterwards I will send for many hunters, and they will hunt them from every mountain and every hill and from the clefts of the rocks'" (Jeremiah 16:16).

God is determined to find the sons of Israel and restore them to the land He gave them. The "hunter" referred to is a "trapper of fowl," a person who captures his quarry alive. While the work of evangelists is usually described in terms of fishing (Matthew 4:19), I find it exciting that hunters can have a hand in helping gather the weary and lost to a life in Christ.

"The lame will leap like a deer" (Isaiah 35:6).

Doesn't that sound joyful! Isaiah 35 describes the desired state of tranquility God promised to Abraham. The passage also describes the peace and abundance we all desire. Healing and restoration will be so complete we'll jump and move like deer.

"These are the animals which you may eat: the ox, the sheep, the goat, the deer, the gazelle, the roe deer, the wild goat, the mountain goat, the antelope, and the mountain sheep. And you may eat every animal with cloven hooves, having the hoof split into two parts, and that chews the cud, among the animals" (Deuteronomy 14:3-8).

An explanation of the reasons God implemented these dietary rules for that time period is beyond the scope of this book. Suffice it to say that I'm profoundly grateful God mentioned critters I like to hunt—especially deer. Amen…and pass the gravy and biscuits!

"Be sober, be vigilant; because your adversary the devil walks about like a roaring lion, seeking whom he may devour" (1 Peter 5:8).

Outdoor analogies ring true with so many of us. We can vividly picture a hungry, roaring lion. The skillful wariness of animals such as elk, deer, and wild turkeys reveal the alertness we need to practice when watching for and avoiding temptation. There's also an inherent caution. These wary animals often abandon their cautious nature during mating seasons, putting themselves at risk—a lesson we shouldn't ignore either.

"And a voice came to him, 'Rise, Peter; kill and eat'" (Acts 10:13).

With a gleam in their eyes I've heard hunters quote this passage as their mandate to arise early and head to deer stands, turkey and duck blinds, and elk and bear country. Although this isn't what this Scripture refers to, my only comment: "Is the alarm set, and did you set a second one just in case?"

"You are my God; early will I seek You" (Psalm 63:1).

As I walk to my deer stand with the sun coming up and the world coming alive around me, this verse reminds me to lift my heart in praise and pursuit of God.

"Till an arrow struck his liver" (Proverbs 7:23).

This verse is about a young man who foolishly was enticed by a prostitute. The resulting spiritual demise is illustrated vividly by an arrow passing through his liver. I wondered why Scripture cites "the liver" until the day I arrowed a deer that way. While the kill was sure, the deer suffered longer than if hit with a heart/lung shot. Avoid temptation!

"Blessed be the name of the LORD from this time forth and forevermore. From the rising of the sun to its going down the LORD's name is to be praised" (Psalm 113:2-3).

Don't you love being in the woods from sunrise to sunset? From where we can see the sun come up to the place we watch it set, from horizon to horizon, is where worship is to happen. Worshiping God takes place all the time and everywhere.

"He has also made Me a select arrow; He has hidden Me in His quiver" (Isaiah 49:2 NASB).

Preparing to enter the woods for an archery hunt includes readying my arrows in terms of broadhead sharpness and shaft straightness. I want flight-worthy arrows in my quiver. These become my "choice" arrows, the ones I depend on for dead-on shots. Isaiah 49:2 is an incredible picture of how much God loves us and is making us His "select" arrows, worthy to be used by Him. The apostle Paul said, "For I am confident of this very thing, that He who began a good work in you will perfect it until the day of Christ Jesus" (Philippians 1:6 NASB).

"In the morning, O LORD, You will hear my voice; in the morning I will order my prayer to You and eagerly watch" (Psalm 5:3 NASB).

A predawn trek to a deer stand, a turkey or duck blind, or the mountains is without question my favorite part of the day. I'm usually rested, plenty excited, and eager to engage in the pursuit of game. The psalmist knew early morning hours were times of mental freshness, perfect for communicating with God. As you eagerly watch for game, also commune with God.

"Their tongue is a deadly arrow; it speaks deceit; with his mouth one speaks peace to his neighbor, but inwardly he sets an ambush for him" (Jeremiah 9:8 NASB).

Hunters know the massive damage arrows can cause. It's humbling to know my words either hurt or heal, harm or encourage harmony, kill or calm. Proverbs 18:21 says, "Death and life are in the power of the tongue." What are your words doing?

"He guides me in the paths of righteousness for His name's sake" (Psalm 23:3).

In the original Hebrew, "paths" meant "tracks." Being guided by God on tracks of righteousness means He's leading me in His purity and holiness. If I step where He steps, I'll be safely guided to my ultimate destination—oneness with Him and being in His presence—and honor His name.

"When the boys grew up, Esau became a skillful hunter, a man of the field; but Jacob was a peaceful [complete] man, living in tents" (Genesis 25:27 NASB).

Esau wasn't born with a bow and quiver in his hand; he learned his hunting skills. He was "a man of the field." Esau ate, slept, and breathed the hunt! But later he sold his birthright, a sure sign that his priorities became skewed. Esau's dedication to hunting inspires me to improve, but I'm also reminded to keep my main focus on those things that are truly important—God and family.

ABOUT THE AUTHOR

Steve's love of hunting began in his early teens on a weekend when one of his dad's church members invited him to tag along on an October squirrel hunt. Archery is his first choice for use in the field, followed by muzzle loader, and then pistol or rifle. To date, according to Steve's calculations, he's entered the woods before daylight on more than a thousand mornings and hopes to continue that trend for many more years.

Proudly claiming West Virginia as his home state, Steve grew up as the son of a preacher. He met his wife, Annie, in junior high school in 1963. In March 1975, they married and settled in Nashville, Tennessee. There they raised their son and daughter, Nathan and Heidi. When Nathan and Heidi met and married their mates, Steve and Annie enthusiastically accepted their new daughter-in-law and son-in-law, and now they dote on the newest member of the family—their granddaughter, Lily.

Steve is president of S&A Family, Inc., an organization formed to oversee the production of the Chapmans' recorded music. They've had "family life" as the theme of their lyrics since they began singing together in 1980. As Dove Award-winning artists, their schedule sends them to more than 100 cities a year to present concerts.

Discography of the Chapman Family

At the Potter's House
An Evening Together
Dogwood…Down the Road
Every Moment
Family Favorites
Finish Well
For Times Like These
Gotta Get There
Hymns from God's Great Cathedral
Kiss of Hearts
Long Enough to Know
Love Was Spoken
The Miles
A Mother's Touch
Nathan Paul
Never Turn Back
Silver Bridge
Steppin' in the Tracks
That Way Again
This House Still Stands
Tools for the Trade
Waiting to Hear

To hear the Chapmans' music, see available
products (CDs/cassettes/videos/books),
find out where they're performing,
or get more information, check out:

www.SteveandAnnieChapman.com

or write to

S &A Family, Inc.
PO Box 337
Madison, TN 37146

A Look at Life from a Deer Stand

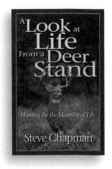

From the incredible rush of bagging "the big one" to standing in awe of God's magnificent creation, avid sportsman Steve Chapman captures the spirit of the hunt. In short chapters filled with excitement and humor, he takes you on his successful and not-so-successful forays into the heart of deer country. As you experience the joy of scouting a trophy buck, you'll discover how the skills necessary for great hunting can help you draw closer to the Lord.

Another Look at Life from a Deer Stand

Drawing on his many years of hunting, Steve takes you to the forests and fields to experience the exhilaration of sighting whitetails and wily turkeys. From the joys of being in the woods to the thrill of handling well-made equipment, you'll relate to the adventure of going after wild game. Along the way you'll also garner some intriguing life truths that will impact your everyday life...spiritual truths that reflect the bounty and grace of the Creator.